813
HAM

**DATE DUE**

| | | | |
|---|---|---|---|
| | | | |
| | | | |
| | | | |
| | | | |
| | | | |
| | | | |
| | | | |
| | | | |
| | | | |
| | | | |
| | | | |
| | | | |
| | | | |

# MASTERS OF HORROR

BY SUE HAMILTON

VISIT US AT

WWW.ABDOPUBLISHING.COM

Published by ABDO Publishing Company, 4940 Viking Drive, Suite 622, Edina, Minnesota 55435.
Copyright ©2007 by Abdo Consulting Group, Inc. International copyrights reserved in all countries.
No part of this book may be reproduced in any form without written permission from the publisher.
ABDO & Daughters™ is a trademark and logo of ABDO Publishing Company.

Printed in the United States.    OCLC: 73140114

**Editors:** John Hamilton/Tad Bornhoft
**Graphic Design:** Sue Hamilton
**Cover Design:** Neil Klinepier
**Cover Illustration:** Stephen King, WireImage
**Interior Photos and Illustrations:** p 1 Lon Chaney, Sr., in *London After Midnight,* courtesy Metro-Goldwyn-Mayer Studios, Inc.; p 4 *Frankenstein* frontispiece, Mary Evans Picture Library; p 5 Mary Shelley, Corbis; p 6 *Murders in the Rue Morgue* poster, courtesy Universal Pictures Corp.; p 7 Edgar Allan Poe, Corbis; p 8 *Dracula* cover, courtesy Doubleday, Page & Co.; p 9 Bram Stoker, Getty Images; p 10 *Weird Tales*, courtesy Popular Fiction Publishing Co.; p 11 H.P. Lovecraft, © Paul Carrick; p 12 Stephen King novels, courtesy Random House Publishing; p 13 Stephen King portrait, courtesy Stephen King; p 14 *Goosebumps* book cover, courtesy Scholastic , Inc.; p 15 R.L. Stine, AP/Wideworld; p 16 Dean Koontz novels, courtesy Random House Publishing; p 17 Dean Koontz, Getty Images; p 18 Pinhead character, AP/Wideworld; p 19 *The Thief Of Always*, courtesy of HarperCollinsPublishers; p 19 Clive Barker, Getty Images; pp 20 and 21 Alfred Hitchcock, Getty Images; p 22 Bela Lugosi photos, courtesy Universal Pictures Corp.; p 23 *Dracula* movie poster, courtesy Universal Pictures Corp.; p 24 Boris Karloff photos from *The Mummy*, courtesy Universal Pictures Corp.; p 25 Boris Karloff as Frankenstein's monster, courtesy Universal Pictures Corp.; p 26 Lon Chaney, Sr., courtesy Universal Pictures Corp.; p 27 *The Wolf Man* poster, courtesy Universal Pictures Corp.; Lon Chaney, Jr., courtesy United Artists; p 28 *The Bat* publicity card, courtesy Allied Artists Pictures Corp.; *House on Haunted Hill* poster, courtesy Allied Artists Pictures Corp.; p 29 Vincent Price, courtesy American International Pictures; p 31 Boris Karloff and Marilyn Harris, courtesy Universal Pictures Corp.

Library of Congress Cataloging-in-Publication Data

Hamilton, Sue L., 1959-
  Masters of horror / Sue Hamilton.
    p. cm. -- (The world of horror)
  Includes index.
  ISBN-13: 978-1-59928-770-6
  ISBN-10: 1-59928-770-6
  1. Horror tales, American--History and criticism--Juvenile literature. 2. Authors, American--Biography--Juvenile literature. 3. Horror tales, English--History and criticism--Juvenile literature. 4. Authors, English--Biography--Juvenile literature. I. Title.
  PS374.H67H36 2007
  813'.0873809
                    2006032737

# CONTENTS

# MARY WOLLSTONECRAFT SHELLEY

*What terrified me will terrify others; and I need only describe the
spectre which had haunted my midnight pillow.*

—Mary Wollstonecraft Shelley

**M**ary Wollstonecraft Shelley was just 19 years old when she finished writing *Frankenstein, or, The Modern Prometheus*. Little did she know that this tale, inspired by a challenge and a sad dream, would make her one of the first authors of modern horror.

Shelley was born to William and Mary Godwin on August 30, 1797, in London, England. Her mother, a feminist author, died a few days after giving birth. Shelley's father, who was also an author, homeschooled "pretty little Mary," emphasizing reading and writing.

In November 1812, Mary first met Percy Bysshe Shelley, an educated and wealthy young poet who visited her father's bookshop and home in London. As the months passed, Percy fell in love with the beautiful and intelligent Mary.

Percy Shelley, who felt trapped in an unhappy marriage, left his pregnant wife to be with Mary in July 1814. However, their union was one of sorrow and death. Mary's father was furious that Mary and Percy had run off together. Within two years, Mary became pregnant twice, but both babies died. Money became an issue when Percy's family did not support the couple.

In 1816, the two went to Switzerland to visit Mary's stepsister, who was with the famous poet Lord George Byron. Many days of rain kept the group inside. To pass the time, they sometimes read ghost stories. Lord Byron challenged them to create their own tales. Mary struggled at first, but a nightmare provided

*Below:* An illustration from Mary Shelley's *Frankenstein,* first published in 1818.

inspiration. She dreamed of a troubled man kneeling beside a creature, a horror created by his own two hands, "the pale student of unhallowed arts kneeling beside the thing he had put together." With this spark of an idea, Shelley feverishly wrote her novel.

*Frankenstein* is a tale about a deranged scientist, Victor Frankenstein, who uses modern technology to create life. Wielding this God-like power, he animates the shell of a creature put together from dead body parts.

Frankenstein recoils in horror at his repulsive experiment. Panic-stricken, the mad scientist runs away. The creature, abandoned and unloved, finally seeks revenge against its creator.

*Above:* Mary Wollstonecraft Shelley, author of *Frankenstein*.

*Frankenstein* became one of the most popular stories of its time. The story is a warning to mankind not to "overreach," not to blindly use new technology without understanding the possible consequences.

Shelley went on to write several more novels and short stories until her death of brain cancer on February 1, 1851. *Frankenstein* was her claim to fame—an undying tale of horror brought to life during a storm.

# EDGAR ALLAN POE

*Poetry is the rhythmical creation of beauty in words.*

—Edgar Allan Poe

*Below:* A poster for the 1932 movie version of Edgar Allan Poe's *The Murders in the Rue Morgue.*

As a master of the macabre, Edgar Allan Poe created eerie poems and short stories that reflected his difficult life. He was born on January 19, 1809, in Boston, Massachusetts. By the time he was two, his father had abandoned the family, and his mother had died of tuberculosis. John and Francis Allan took the boy in. His middle name reflects the name of his foster parents.

In February 1826, having just turned 17 years old, Poe entered the University of Virginia. A talented writer and a good student, he unfortunately began gambling to pay his bills. His father refused to pay off the resulting debt. Poe was forced to leave the university in December.

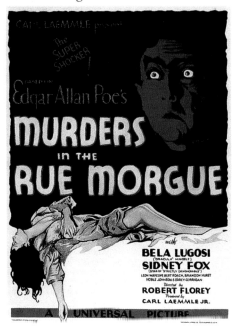

In 1827, Poe published his first book of poems, entitled *Tamerlane and Other Poems by A Bostonian.* This brought in little money, so Poe entered the United States Army under the name Edgar A. Perry. Two years later, he entered the U.S. Military Academy at West Point. He remained at the elite school only a few months, but his fellow cadets helped the popular author publish *Poems by Edgar A. Poe.*

In 1835, Poe married his first cousin, Virginia, a girl of 13. He supported her by editing magazines, and by writing fiction. Poe penned *The Unparalleled Adventure of One Hans Pfaal,* a science fiction story of travel to the moon, as well as *The Murders in the Rue Morgue,* often considered the first modern "detective" story.

But it was Poe's gruesome stories and sadly rhythmical poetry that made him a legend. His great works are popular even today: *The Fall of the House of Usher* (1840), *The Pit and the Pendulum* (1842), *The Tell-Tale Heart* (1843), and especially the poem that some consider his masterpiece, *The Raven,* published in 1845.

On October 3, 1849, a feverish Poe was found lying on a street in Baltimore, Maryland. He died four days later in a hospital, unable to explain what had happened to him. His death remains a mystery. His gravestone carries his most famous words, "Quoth the Raven: 'Nevermore.'"

*Above:* Author Edgar Allan Poe.

# BRAM STOKER

*I have learned not to think little of anyone's belief, no matter how strange it may be. I have tried to keep an open mind, and it is not the ordinary things of life that could close it, but the strange things, the extraordinary things, the things that make one doubt if they be mad or sane.*

—Bram Stoker

Bram Stoker's frightening masterpiece of the "undead" was 1897's *Dracula*. The frightening novel made the author a horror legend. But he began his life in a much less powerful way.

Abraham "Bram" Stoker was born on November 8, 1847, in Dublin, Ireland. A series of illnesses made him bed-ridden until he was nearly seven years old. His parents educated and entertained the boy with stories of the theater, and of life experiences such as the 1832 cholera epidemic in Ireland. This was an odd mixture of information for a creative boy.

Leaving sickness behind, Stoker grew into a champion athlete at Trinity College in Dublin. He won awards in science, math, and debate. After graduation, Stoker worked as a civil servant at Dublin Castle. While there, he wrote his first book, *Duties of Clerks of Petty Sessions in Ireland.*

Stoker found that he enjoyed creative writing. He volunteered as a theater critic for his local newspaper. One column included a glowing review of actor and producer Henry Irving's version of William Shakespeare's *Hamlet.* Irving read Stoker's review, and the two became friends. Stoker went to work as Irving's business manager. Shortly afterward, Bram began writing fiction.

In 1890, Stoker read *The Vampyre,* a short story by John Polidori. This inspired him to create his own book of the undead. Cleverly written in the form of journals and letters from the main characters, *Dracula* was published in 1897 to worldwide success.

Stoker wrote horror and mystery novels until his death on April 20, 1912. None of his other stories came close to the undying success of his masterpiece. In print and film, Bram Stoker's *Dracula* has remained alive for more than 100 years.

*Below:* Bram Stoker's *Dracula.* Originally published in 1897, this edition was printed in 1902. The famous vampire novel has remained in print for more than 100 years.

*Above:* Abraham "Bram" Stoker wrote many horror and mystery novels, but none would be as popular as *Dracula*.

# H.P. LOVECRAFT

*Men of broader intellect know that there is no sharp distinction
betwixt the real and the unreal... .*

—H.P. Lovecraft

H.P. Lovecraft was a 20th-century writer who combined
mystery, horror, and science fiction into a weird blend of
stories. His work influenced the careers of many famous
authors and artists, including Robert Block, Clive Barker,
and Stephen King.

Howard Phillips Lovecraft was born on August 20, 1890,
in Providence, Rhode Island. He could read and write by age 6.
Scientifically curious and highly intelligent, he taught himself
chemistry and astronomy.

In 1898, Lovecraft's father died. He and his mother moved in
with her father, Whipple Van Buren Phillips, who was a wealthy
businessman. Lovecraft and his grandfather got along amazingly
well. The elderly man often told his creative grandson weird tales
of horror. Lovecraft, in turn, created his own odd tales, often
inspired by nightmares. He also wrote science articles.

In 1904, Lovecraft's grandfather died; the family suffered
a huge emotional and financial loss. Lovecraft and his mother
moved into a much smaller residence. It was a sad time for the
young man.

Often ill and alone, Lovecraft never received a high school
diploma, yet he continued to learn and study. He was invited
to join the United Amateur Press Association. This connection
ended his loneliness and created many long-time friends. The
group's encouragement helped him write such tales as *The Tomb*
and *Dagon* in 1917.

Shortly after his mother's death in 1921, Lovecraft attended
an amateur journalism convention, where he met Sonia Greene.
The two were married in 1924 in New York City. For a time, all
was good. Lovecraft's stories were regularly published in the pulp
magazine *Weird Tales.*

*Below:* The
September 1925
issue of *Weird
Tales* contained
H.P. Lovecraft's
short story,
"The Temple."

*Left:* An illustration of horror author H.P. Lovecraft, with one of his monstrous fictional characters.

Sadly, the marriage did not last. Lovecraft returned to his hometown of Providence. There, he wrote some of his best fiction, including *The Call of Cthulhu* and *At the Mountains of Madness*. He also carried on his friendships by writing hundreds of letters.

After his death on March 15, 1937, at the age of 46, his friends put together a volume of his stories. The first edition of *The Outsider and Others* was published in 1939, two years after his death. Lovecraft lives on in his weirdly clever tales of horror and science fiction.

# STEPHEN KING

*People want to know why I do this, why I write such gross stuff. I like to tell them I have the heart of a small boy... and I keep it in a jar on my desk.*

—Stephen King

*Below:* A Random House edition of three classic Stephen King novels.

**STEPHEN KING**

CARRIE

'SALEM'S LOT

THE SHINING

THREE COMPLETE NOVELS

Known as the King of Horror, Stephen King made his mark through clever storytelling in a wonderfully nightmarish way. Stephen Edwin King was born in Portland, Maine, on September 21, 1947. In 1959, King found a box of old books, including Bram Stoker's *Dracula*. He loved horror and science fiction, and decided to write his own tales.

King went to the University of Maine, in Orono, Maine. It was there that he met Tabitha Spruce. The two were married on January 2, 1971. The couple struggled to make ends meet. King worked as an English teacher, and wrote in his spare time on nights and weekends.

Tabitha, who is also an author, never let King stop writing. When he threw a story into the trash about a teenage girl with telekinetic powers, Tabitha fished it out and made him finish the book. *Carrie* became King's first success. Published in 1974, the novel was made into a film two years later. It is one of the few horror films to be nominated for multiple Academy Awards.

King created many more horror tales, several of which became successful box office hits. His second novel, *'Salem's Lot*, which was published in 1975, became his own modern take on the Dracula stories he read as a boy. He published so many stories that he even began writing under a pseudonym, Richard Bachman.

In June 1999, while walking alone on a rural Maine road, King was struck by a car. The accident left him in great pain. The popular author thought he'd never write again, but he made an eventual recovery. In 2001, King published *Dreamcatcher,* which included a character recovering from a car wreck.

In 2003, the National Book Awards gave King a Lifetime Achievement Award. The King of Horror continues his legacy of terror, and millions of readers love shuddering over his every word.

*Below:* Author Stephen King.

# R.L. STINE

*I feel happy to terrify kids.*

—R.L. Stine

Millions of kids today thrill to R.L. Stine's creepy tales of things that go bump in the night. As one of the bestselling children's authors of all time, he now has more than 300 million books in print. However, it took 20 years before success scratched at the popular author's door.

Robert Lawrence Stine was born on October 8, 1943, in Columbus, Ohio. He grew up listening to mysteries on the radio, reading science fiction stories, and pouring over *Tales From The Crypt* comic books. At nine years old, the discovery of a dusty typewriter in the attic started him writing. His fingers tapped out pages of scary fiction and jokes. He later said, "...there's a very close tie between humor and horror."

Stine graduated from Ohio State University in 1965 and then went to work. Writing as Jovial Bob Stine for Scholastic's teen magazine *Bananas,* he created jokes and goofy articles. This led to his first book, *How To Be Funny: An Extremely Silly Guide*, published in 1978.

In the mid-1980s, Stine began freelance writing. His first teen horror novel, *Blind Date*, became a bestseller in 1986. Soon he was working on *Fear Street*, an entire series of teenage horror books.

Younger kids loved these books, too. The author had a ready audience for his *Goosebumps* books—named after Stine saw a listing in *TV Guide* for "Goosebumps Week." The first book in the series, *Welcome to Dead House,* was published in 1992. Another 62 books followed, plus a TV series, movies, and even comic books.

Stine's scary writing caused some controversy. Many adults said his tales were too frightening for children. But no one could argue with the fact that his horror stories helped thousands of kids become avid readers.

Said Stine, "I think everyone likes a good scare, and I think everyone likes to be able to have creepy adventures and face monsters when they know they're safe at the same time."

*Facing Page:* Author R.L. Stine poses with a model skeleton at his New York home in August 2000. *Below:* The first book in Stine's *Goosebumps* series, *Welcome to Dead House.*

# DEAN KOONTZ

*Sometimes there is no darker place than our thoughts,
the moonless midnight of the mind.*

—Dean Koontz

*Below:* A collection of Dean Koontz novels.

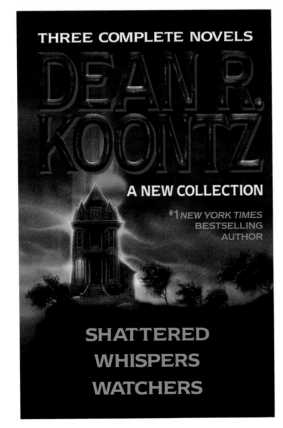

THREE COMPLETE NOVELS

DEAN R. KOONTZ

A NEW COLLECTION

#1 *NEW YORK TIMES*
BESTSELLING
AUTHOR

SHATTERED
WHISPERS
WATCHERS

Suspense, terror, excitement, and fear mark bestselling-author Dean Koontz's books and life. Born Dean Ray Koontz on July 9, 1945, in Everett, Pennsylvania, his youth was marred by an abusive, alcoholic father. At age 8, he set aside his problems to create his own 5¢ hand-written "books." Four years later, his writing won him $25 in a national essay contest. As a senior at Shippensburg State College in Pennsylvania, Koontz won a fiction contest. After graduation, he ended up supporting himself with jobs that only left nights and weekends for writing.

On October 15, 1966, he married Gerda Ann Cerra, who offered to support him for five years while he worked on his books. When the time was up, Koontz was not only a success, but Gerda had become his business manager.

Koontz's first book, *Star Quest*, was published in 1968. Only three years later, the author was nominated for a Hugo Award for *Beastchild*. Suddenly, he was one of the year's best science fiction and fantasy authors.

Koontz wanted to write more than science fiction, so he started using pseudonyms. He wrote as K.R. Dwyer for suspense, David Axton for adventure, Leigh Nichols for romantic suspense, plus several others.

It was Koontz's 1980 novel, *Whispers*, that screamingly flung him into successful suspense writing. This book, like many of his others, featured a madman and a strong woman, characters who were similar to his own father and mother.

Koontz's books often end in a happily-ever-after scenario—just like the author's own life. With over a dozen bestselling novels, Koontz's work has been translated into 38 languages. The man who had so much to overcome is now America's most popular suspense novelist.

*Above:* Author Dean Koontz on his porch in 1998.

# CLIVE BARKER

*Be regular and orderly in your life, that you may be violent and original in your work.*

—Clive Barker

As an author, artist, and film producer, Clive Barker crafts nightmarish creations that have earned him the title "Prince of Horror." Born on October 5, 1952, in Liverpool, England, Barker grew up hearing and telling stories. He learned at an early age that he loved to scare people, and he was good at it.

At first, Barker wanted to be a painter, but his parents told him he couldn't make money doing that. He ended up studying English literature and philosophy. When he was 21 years old, he formed a theater group called the Dog Company. He wrote such plays as *History of the Devil* and *Frankenstein in Love*, and then went on to direct and often act in them as well.

Playwriting led Barker to create short stories. These were published in 1984 in *Books of Blood*. With such titles as "The Midnight Meat Train" and "Dread," the gory tales featured unexpected twists and turns. Barker even illustrated the first English edition's cover.

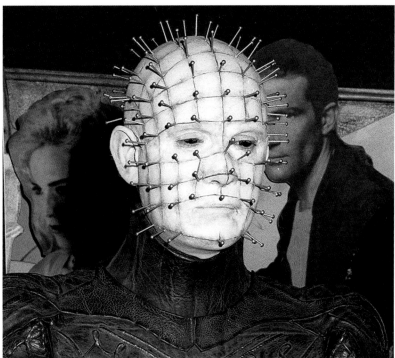

*Below:* Actor Doug Bradley dressed in full "Pinhead" costume and makeup.

Experienced horror author Stephen King gave a boost to the young writer with the often-quoted remark, "I have seen the future of horror and its name is Clive Barker." Barker published two more volumes in the series.

Barker's first full-length novel was published in 1985. The creepy story was about a wealthy man versus a centuries-old creature. The book was filled with blood and terror. Readers squirmed in horror—and loved it.

With this success, Barker wrote and directed his first movie in 1987. The movie

*Above:* Author Clive Barker.
*Below right: The Thief of Always* book cover.

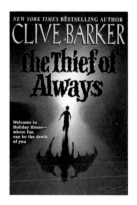

is most remembered for the frightening character dubbed "Pinhead." It became a cult classic, and over the next 20 years, seven more movies were produced in the series.

Clive Barker continues to create movies, plays, and comic books reaching from horror to fantasy. In 2002, he created his first children's book, *The Thief of Always*, mastering a new area of writing and even illustrating many of the pages. A dark genius, his over-the-top storytelling fills readers with the unexpected, the eerie, and the truly bizarre.

# ALFRED HITCHCOCK

*Always make the audience suffer as much as possible.*

—Alfred Hitchcock

**K**nown as the "Master of Suspense," Alfred Hitchcock was one of the most innovative filmmakers of all time. He was born on August 13, 1899, in London, England. At the age of five, his father once punished him by sending him to a police station. Locked in a cell for 10 minutes, young Alfred was terrified. He never forgot that feeling of fear.

Hitchcock graduated from the School for Engineering and Navigation, but became interested in photography. He went to work for Islington Studios in 1920, where he met his future wife, Alma. In 1927, he directed his first breakthrough feature film, *The Lodger*. This black-and-white silent movie was a creepy tale of "The Avenger," a serial killer who terrorized women on the streets of London. It became a huge hit for the 28-year-old director, starting Hitchcock off on his career in suspense films.

In the late 1930s, Hitchcock moved to America. His first Hollywood film, *Rebecca*, came out in 1940, and won an Academy Award for Best Picture. From there, Hitchcock directed everything from comedies (*Mr. & Mrs. Smith)* to thrillers (*North by Northwest*), to horror pictures (*The Birds),* working with all the top stars. His films were often about innocent people swept up in circumstances beyond their control. His themes of fear and guilt were woven within plots that featured blood-curdling suspense.

*Below:* Director Alfred Hitchcock, 1965.

Hitchcock was also known for his dry humor. In each of his films, he made a brief cameo appearance. Audiences made a game of being the first to spot the director in his movies.

Television also offered the clever director opportunities to show off his talent. From 1955 to 1965, he hosted *Alfred Hitchcock Presents.* His distinctive shape and voice became known around the world.

After a lifetime of success in entertaining millions, the director was knighted in 1980, becoming Sir Alfred Joseph Hitchcock. He died a few months later, on April 28, but his dramatic filmmaking became a model for many suspense and drama pictures that followed.

*Above:* Alfred Hitchcock in 1963, posing with some feathered fiends from *The Birds.* *Below:* The famous Hitchcock logo.

# Bela Lugosi

*Every actor's greatest ambition is to create his own, definite and original role—but I found this to be almost fatal.*

—Bela Lugosi

Bela Lugosi was a screen legend who gave a face and voice to the character of Dracula, the vampire. The talented actor was born on October 20, 1882, in Lugos, Austria-Hungary (now Romania). His real name was Béla Ferenc Dezsö Blaskó. His father was a banker, but Bela grew up with an interest in acting. While young, he took the stage name of Bela Lugosi.

In 1917, Lugosi performed in his first film, *Az Ezredes (The Colonel).* He went on to successful work in many films in Hungary and Germany.

Lugosi moved to the United States in 1920. His heavily-accented voice made it difficult for him to find work, but in 1927 his fate changed when he took the lead role for the stage play *Dracula.* When Universal Pictures decided to produce

*Below Left:* Bela Lugosi. *Below Right:* Lugosi in his famous role in Universal Pictures' 1931 *Dracula.*

the film version three years later, Lugosi convinced the director and producer that he was right for the role. Released in 1931 to great success, *Dracula* launched Lugosi's horror-movie career, which lasted more than 25 years.

With his heavy Hungarian accent and distinctive look, Lugosi, for better or worse, was typecast by Hollywood into low-budget B-movies. Audiences of the 1930s and 1940s loved the sinister films, which included such titles as *Murders in the Rue Morgue* (1932), *Mark of the Vampire* (1935), and *The Black Cat* (1941).

As the years passed, Lugosi found it more and more difficult to get

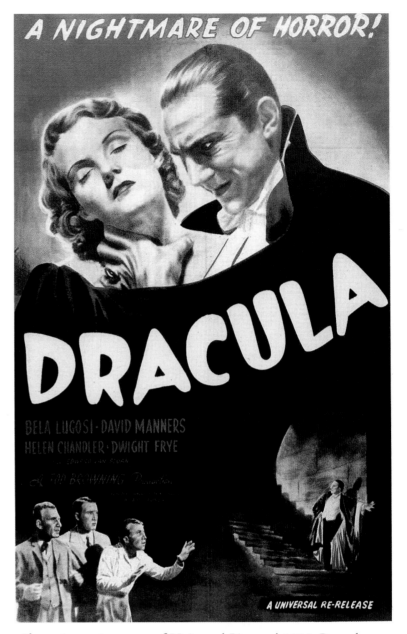

*Above:* A movie poster of Universal Pictures' 1931 *Dracula.*

decent roles. He often was reduced to playing his Dracula character in comedies. Due to back injuries, he became addicted to painkillers, which made it even more difficult for him to find work.

Bela Lugosi died of a heart attack on August 16, 1956. In fitting style, he was buried wearing his Dracula cape. While his later years were marred with difficulty, it is impossible to erase the impact he made as one of the masters of horror.

# BORIS KARLOFF

*The monster was the best friend I ever had.*
—Boris Karloff

*Above:* Boris Karloff in 1932's *The Mummy.*

**B**oris Karloff, who was often billed as "Karloff the Uncanny," made his fame in cinema playing Frankenstein, the Mummy, Dr. Jekyll and Mr. Hyde, and many more frightening characters of horror.

Born William Henry Pratt on November 23, 1887, in London, England, he took an interest in acting as a young man. In 1909, he moved to Canada to pursue his career. He changed his name to the exotic-sounding "Boris Karloff," and soon became a popular on-stage villain.

Future work landed Karloff in the United States. Tall and thin with a slow, menacing step, his big break came in 1930 when director James Whale cast him as the monster in *Frankenstein,* a part turned down by horror superstar Bela Lugosi. When *Frankenstein* was released in 1931, Boris Karloff became an overnight sensation.

*Below:* After eight hours of make-up, Boris Karloff plays the terrifying Egyptian mummy, Imhotep.

In 1932's *The Mummy,* Karloff was cast as Imhotep, an ancient Egyptian priest searching for his lost love. The patient Karloff endured an agonizing transformation. Thin cotton strips were glued to his face, at which point Karloff could no longer speak. Next came a thick layer of clay, cracks painstakingly hand-carved into the drying muck. Makeup paint came next. Finally, Karloff was wrapped in 150 yards (137 m) of ragged linen. Eight hours later, he was ready for another eight hours of work filming the movie.

*Left:* Karloff in his role as the monster in *Frankenstein.* The 1931 movie made Boris Karloff famous.

The difficult work paid off. *The Mummy* was a huge hit for Karloff and Universal Pictures. It would be one of many successes for the talented actor.

Despite his frightening on-screen persona, Boris Karloff was known for his generosity to charities and kindness to children. In 1966, at the age of 79, he famously narrated the classic animated show, *How The Grinch Stole Christmas.*

From movies to television to comics, Karloff was immediately recognizable. He died on February 2, 1969, but his dramatic performances have made him an everlasting master of horror.

# LON CHANEY, SR.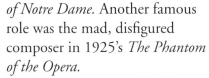

*Between pictures, there is no Lon Chaney.*

—Lon Chaney, Sr.

*Below:* Lon Chaney, Sr., in *The Phantom of the Opera.* The talented Chaney did his own make-up for his roles.

Known as the "Man of a Thousand Faces," Lon Chaney, Sr., worked on many silent films in the early 20th century. He was born on April 1, 1883, in Colorado Springs, Colorado. His real name was Leonidas Frank Chaney. His parents could neither speak nor hear. He grew up using pantomime, facial expressions, and sign language to communicate. These skills benefited him greatly, both on stage and in the era of silent movies.

Chaney took many varied roles, but became famous for his work as Quasimodo, the hunchback in 1923's *The Hunchback of Notre Dame.* Another famous role was the mad, disfigured composer in 1925's *The Phantom of the Opera.*

He was a master of make-up, changing himself into whatever role he took on. From a tragic clown to a man-ape creature, Chaney knew how to make himself look the part. In fact, Chaney's own face was so rarely seen that he could go out in public and not be recognized.

In 1930, the 47-year-old's last picture, *The Unholy Three,* showed the talented actor's ability to use different voices. Sadly, just as talking pictures were becoming popular, Chaney—a long-time smoker—died of cancer on August 26, 1930.

Luckily for Hollywood, Lon Chaney had a son who followed in his father's masterful footsteps.

# LON CHANEY, JR.

*Of course I believe that* The Wolf Man *is the best of my horror films—because he is mine!*
—Lon Chaney, Jr.

*Right:* A publicity poster for *The Wolf Man.*
*Below:* Lon Chaney, Jr., as Lennie, the mentally challenged giant, in *Of Mice and Men.*

Creighton Tull Chaney was born February 10, 1906, in Oklahoma City, Oklahoma. His parents, Lon Chaney and Frances Bush, were both actors. Even though his father tried to stop him, Creighton entered the movie business.

At 6′ 2″ (1.88 m) tall, Creighton started work as a stunt man, but found himself cast in several rolls as a villain. He received excellent reviews as Lennie, a mentally challenged man, in the classic 1939 movie, *Of Mice and Men.* He might have had a serious movie career, but Universal Pictures decided the time was right for more horror films. To build on his father's legacy, the young actor followed the studio's advice and changed his name to Lon Chaney, Jr.

*The Wolf Man* was released in 1941 to great popular success. From there, Chaney starred in such horror movies as *The Ghost of Frankenstein* (1942), *Son of Dracula* (1943), *The Mummy's Ghost* (1944), and many more.

Chaney worked on hundreds of movies and television programs until his death on July 12, 1973. He enjoyed renewed popularity with audiences in his later years when his classic horror movies were aired on television. Like his father before him, Lon Chaney, Jr., became a master of horror.

# VINCENT PRICE

*It's as much fun to scare as to be scared.*

—Vincent Price

*Facing Page:*
Vincent Price
holds the wax
head of actor
Peter Lorre from
*Tales of Terror.*
*Right:* A publicity
card for *The Bat.*
*Below: House on*
*Haunted Hill*
starred Vincent
Price as the host
of a deadly party.

Dubbed the "Merchant of Menace," Vincent Price had a deeply eerie voice and a sinister laugh that sent shivers down the spine. Vincent Leonard Price, Jr., was born on May 27, 1911. His father, Vincent Price, Sr., was president of the National Candy Company in St. Louis, Missouri. Young Vincent's life was filled with everything money could buy.

Price went to Yale University in the 1930s, and took an interest in theater. At 6′ 4″ (1.93 m) tall, his commanding presence and strong voice landed him a number of roles.

In the 1940s Price moved to Hollywood, California, working in film and radio. This eventually led him to horror films in the 1950s. Starring in Warner Brothers' first 3D film, *House of Wax*, Price played a murderous sculptor who displayed his victims' wax-covered bodies in his museum. Immensely successful at the box office, the film became the year's fourth-biggest grossing movie. Price was on his way to becoming a horror star and the "King of 3D."

In the 1960s, Price became famous for his work in several movies based on the stories of Edgar Allen Poe, including *The Pit and the Pendulum* and *The Raven.*

Although Price went on to play dozens of roles, his unique look and voice often cast him as a villain. In 1983, Price narrated singer Michael Jackson's immensely popular horror music video, *Thriller.* In 1990, at the age of 79, he played the inventor of actor Johnny Depp's title character, Edward Scissorhands.

Vincent Price died of lung cancer on October 25, 1993. He was a modern master of horror who will always be fondly remembered for his unique voice, look, and haunting laugh.

# GLOSSARY

**B-MOVIE**
A Hollywood motion picture originally meant to run as the second half of a double feature. B-movies were usually less flashy, with cheaper budgets, and were often genre films such as Westerns, horror, or science fiction.

**CAMEO**
A minor role played by a well-known actor in a movie. Such a part is often limited to a single scene.

**CHOLERA**
A severe, often fatal intestinal disease transmitted by contaminated water or food. Worldwide, several cities with inadequate sewer systems and crowded housing districts experienced cholera epidemics in the 19th century.

**HUGO AWARD**
The annual award presented by the World Science Fiction Society to honor the year's best science fiction. Named after the legendary writer and editor Hugo Gernsback, who founded the magazine *Amazing Stories* in 1926.

**PANTOMIME**
A method of conveying emotions, actions, and feelings using gestures and facial expressions without speech. A pantomime is also a play or sketch in which actors are mute and express themselves only through gestures.

**PSEUDONYM**
A false name used by an author to conceal his or her identity. Also called a pen name.

**SHAKESPEARE, WILLIAM**
William Shakespeare, 1564-1616, was an English playwright and poet whose works are considered among the greatest in English literature. Known as "the Bard," Shakespeare's plays include *Hamlet* and *Romeo and Juliet.*

**TELEKINETIC**
The alleged ability to move or deform objects without physical contact, as if through a mental process.

### TUBERCULOSIS

An infectious and potentially fatal disease that most often affects the lungs, but may spread to other areas of the body. The disease is caused by bacteria, and is commonly spread through coughing.

### TYPECAST

An actor is typecast when he or she is repeatedly cast in similar character roles following the actor's first successful movie appearance. Being typecast may provide steady work, but becoming so strongly identified with a particular role can limit an actor's opportunities.

### UNDEAD

A reanimated body of a dead person. A part of stories and legends in many cultures, the undead appear in different forms such as ghosts, vampires, or zombies.

*Above:* In this famous scene from the 1931 film *Frankenstein,* Boris Karloff's monster is befriended by a little girl played by Marilyn Harris.

# INDEX